CHRIST UNVE

HIS HEAVENLY &

EARTHLY APPEARING

(1887)

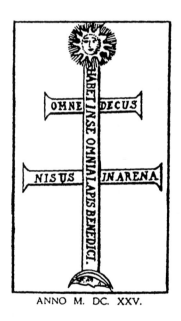

ANNO M. DC. XXV.

Anna J. Johnson

ISBN 0-7661-0228-9

KESSINGER PUBLISHING, LLC

http://www.kessingerpub.com

email: books@kessingerpub.com

CHRIST UNVEILED:

HIS

HEAVENLY AND EARTHLY

APPEARING.

BY

ANNA J. JOHNSON,

AUTHOR OF "THE HEALING VOICE."

———

NEW YORK:

PRESS OF JAS. N. JOHNSTON, 22 BEEKMAN STREET.

1887.

Yours Sincerely

THE FOLLOWING PAGES ARE
INSCRIBED
To My Beloved Daughter,
IN ACKNOWLEDGEMENT OF HER AFFECTION AND
FAITHFUL LOYALTY TO HER MOTHER,
AMID MANY
TRANSITIONS AND TRIALS.

PREFACE.

JESUS said to His Apostles, Ye shall receive power after that the Holy Ghost is come upon you ; and ye shall be witness unto me both in Jerusalem, and in Samaria, and unto the uttermost parts of the earth. And when Jesus had spoken these things, while they beheld, He was taken up, and a cloud received him out of their sight. And while they looked stead-fastly towards Heaven as He went up, behold, two men stood by them in white apparel, which also said, Ye men of Gallilee, why stand ye gazing up into Heaven? This same Jesus shall so come in like manner as ye have seen Him go into Heaven. Acts 1.

In accordance with the written word, the writer confesses and testifies boldly, that this same Jesus has been her personal Saviour, the Teacher and Revelator from Heaven to her ; and that her faith has become sight, and her hope of Heaven a blessed reality. These revelations she gives now to the world in His name, and in His will.

CONTENTS.

INTRODUCTORY.

THIS book is given to the world as revelations and prophesies from the Lord. It carries the message of glad tidings to the children of men, especially to the lost sheep of the house of Israel. It calls all to come to the marriage supper of the Lamb. It supplies the wedding garment to all who are called to the feast. It simplifies the way of salvation, making the path of each easy and the burden light. It gives the law and the gospel of all religions. It interprets all tongues. It embraces all truths, and all life in its separate order and degree. It holds the balances by which each soul can weigh itself, and become its own interpreter of law and gospel. Comprehending therefore, the weights and measures of a just God—a wise Creator—He who calls for only that which His people can give, and that which is His to receive, when He calls for it. The life that is given by the Creator to all is spirit, which must return to Him in time, bearing the evidences of the use or misuse which each one has made of it. This book is written and given to the world by one who has passed through the righteous judgments of Heaven, and has therefore nothing to fear from the judgments of earth. It carries to all the olive branch of peace, the positive proof that the waters of the world have abated, and that the ark of God's covenant rests solidly in one human soul. We hope and pray that this volume may carry the spirit of love and truth to all God's people, enabling each one to see Christ not only in the clouds of Heaven, but as the life of their own soul and body, the Saviour of the life of each, the Restorer of all that has been lost in the wilderness of error, doubt and uncertainty, since the creation of man.

May the holy spirit quicken the soul and mind of all who read this book, and may His spirit bring to the author very many hearts in spiritual unison and understanding with her own, that God's children may come together, prepared to stand as pillars in the temple of our God. Those who have ripened in the school of Christ, in the vineyard of the Lord, will readily perceive the spirit revealed in this book. Those who have not added to their faith, knowledge, may stumble until the holy spirit gives understanding. Dear reader, let the spirit of truth teach you, ere you reject the revelations and prophesies of this book. Truths given beyond your

experience cannot harm you, but may stimulate
your heart and mind and become healthful food to
the soul, remembering the promise "that when the
truth makes you free, you are free indeed."

After fifteen years and over in God's service,
walking in His will, having His spirit witnessing
with mine, teaching and revealing to me the laws
of life, and how to conform to these laws; and in
Christ becoming reconciled to all law, and in Him
overcoming the natural restrictions in life; understanding through severe experiences, the individual
environment which surrounds all under the different
degrees of grace during the human growth of physical
and spiritual development. I can now in His will, say,
that the spirit of the law of life in Christ Jesus has
made me free from the law of sin and death. I realize
God's word; "I will ransom them from the power
of the grave." "O Death, I will be thy plague"
"O Grave, I will be thy destruction," Hosea 13,
14. Dear reader, I can now say in spirit and in
truth, "Our Father who art in Heaven, hallowed
by Thy name, Thy Kingdom come, Thy will be
done on earth as in Heaven." This consciousness
in one's self brings the individual idea to where it
knows God, and to know God is to know self fully,
and to have the eyes of your understanding opened

to the all of things—the seen and the unseen—" the Lord of earth and Heaven." "He that revealeth secrets that maketh known to thee what shall come to pass."

THE VEIL LIFTED.

SINCE the evening of May 3d, 1871, Christ Jesus has talked with me. He reveals to me the natural and the spirit world; the life of each and the relation of the one to the other. It was shown me that all life came out from God in the beginning, perfect, that is the life-principle in the procreative law was perfect, and, as it was in the beginning, it now is, and always will be to the end of time. In this life-principle there is the male and female germ, or seed, from which springs the natural form, or human nature of each; also that each human soul contains the divine principle of a dual nature. From this divine law spring the natural form of life, also the spiritual; but owing to ignorance of this parent, or original seed, we naturally look for only a human development, well formed bone, muscle, nerve and sinew; also a well developed brain, capable of being taught by the highest intelligence of enlightened minds so as to comprehend the laws of natural sciences, for by this proper training the mental and physical forces of life are developed to their fullest capacity. This is as far, therefore, as the natural sciences can enlighten.

Thus when man attains to his full knowledge as an intellectual man, he is only an educated animal. As the Divine Spirit has never been quickened, it is in its germinal state. This animal man, refined and polished, may be even intellectually clear on spiritual subjects, yet entirely ignorant of the original seed, or life-principle from whence he came. His, or her knowledge of spiritual things having come to them through education or association with those deeply imbued with veneration, and a love of purity and truth ; having an aspiration to attain towards what they have been taught to believe to be, God's requirements. Consequently we find the principle of law and order, justice, purity and truth, often visibly manifested in some people according to Scripture, as the laws written on their hearts. " The engrafted word." This is the result of spiritual enlightenment, the educational training of one generation having been handed down to the next. Thus we see that the engrafted religious spirit of the past, is principally resulting in idealism in the present day; which has come to different ones through their emotional nature, or the study of the Word of God; as mental science is studied with a view of teach-

ing it to others. Clergymen and teachers who through
natural study, explain and define God's word from
their natural capacity to comprehend it; altho' they
admit that God is so far beyond them that it is
impossible to know Him, yet their hearers one after
another catch up their ideas, and finally a natural
conclusion is formed for the mind of others to rest
upon. This is largely seen in the denominationalism
of to-day. No church has attained its fullness, or
ripened state of perfection, until each individual
member has learned and lived the Lord's Prayer, and
studied the message given by the beloved John to
the seven churches.

It was a spiritual message from the Lord through
John to His people, in the churches, yet individually
to every human soul, so that we must understand its
individual relation to one and all. The natural man
is told in the Scriptures that his body is Christ's
house, and that there is a spirit in man, and the inspiration of the Almighty giveth it understanding;
also, that God made man in His own image, male
and female, and blessed them. His spirit works in
the human soul to will and to do of His own good
pleasure. Man is told in the Scriptures to examine
himself and see whether this faith be in him; to
prove himself and also to know that the spirit of

Jesus Christ is in him, or else he is a reprobate,
(which means one who has lived in his carnal nature,
having put from him all spiritual light).

When a soul has proved himself and admitted
God's right to rule the life of soul and body, God's
Spirit becomes the Saviour, Teacher and Guide
of his natural and spiritual life.   Man is then under a Tutor, one who knows all flesh, all nature, and
all the varied vicissitudes of life, under the micro-
scope of the Eternal Eye, of the Great Master Mind
of the Universe, to whom all human nature must
submit, in its progressive state of unfoldment, or
rather in its attaining to the perfected state required
in the message of God to the people through the
divine revelator, St. John.   This Holy Spirit teaches
man to know himself and his relation to his God.
It teaches man the natural attributes, revealing the
spiritual man, as the interior life of man, showing
that man is dual, having a double or two-fold nature,
which is male and female, positive and negative,
natural and spiritual.   In the natural man we have,
the seven senses, the seven principles or pre-
cepts of God to be unfolded in the soul, mind and
body.   First, there are the five natural senses, seeing, hearing, tasting, smelling and feeling.   Each of
these are to be developed to the fullest extent—

that is, sight, strong and clear; hearing, distinct, so that no sound can escape observation within the range of human sound; so it must be with smell, taste and touch. Then there is the sixth sense, the intuitive—that still small voice, which speaks to each one in solitude where no eye nor ear sees or hears, what passes between the still small voice and the human soul.

This sixth sense is the avenue of the Holy Spirit, called the spirit of truth, the Teacher and Revelator from the Lord. Its office work is to guide the natural mind in matters of real duty, of equity and justice. It is like the needle in the compass. It points out the true course to take. It warns us always when we consult it by revealing the danger signals all along the path of life. This is one of the great good lessons taught us by the still small voice. Then again it might be likened to a central sun in the soul, which enlightens the natural mind continually, illuminating the natural faculties, bringing all the natural forces under the clear observatory of the balances of human reason and justice, testing and comparing the degree of uniform unfoldment of each of the five senses. By these five senses, spiritually illustrated, we are enabled to look in and through our interior being; it is the candle of God;

to each one, it has its own peculiar relationship to the earthly house. From this sense centre, located in the brain, there are to each of the five senses lines of corresponding nerves and muscles, bearing messages to all parts of the body, conducted direct or by and through the nerve centres, so that if one sense or member suffers, all the other senses and parts are affected by it.

The sixth sense is likened to a master mechanic, who superintends all the office work of one and all of the natural senses; each watched over and attended to, very much as a gardener watches over his different varieties of plants and shrubs; giving to each, water, air and sunshine according to its need.

"I am the true Vine, and my Father the husbandman."—St. John, xv.

Thus it is with our progressive growth in human development, until each sense has attained its perfected state, where the spirit of the sixth sense rules and regulates harmoniously the five natural senses, and through them, all the faculties of the mind and members of the body. This brings the human will, and the purposes of that will, under the entire control of the Holy Spirit, thus the spirit holds the supreme control of the natural body.

This gives the Holy Spirit the ascendency, so

that it uses the natural house for its personating of the spirit of love and wisdom, in words, in works, in manifested power, to the extent of all truth, on all subjects of truth, and all lines of truth, giving a definite response or reply to all Scripture, making a sure foundation on which to place God's word, that we may see and feel the manifestation of His power within us at all times.

This knowledge is the needed want of the people, so as to have the *witness of the spirit of truth* in themselves, to be so *entirely the Lord's* that they are the representative, personal church to whom St. John's message was given—"No other foundation can any man lay than that which is laid, being Jesus Christ, the chief corner-stone." This personal spirit of truth in oneself is the witness in the earth, with that which is in the Heavens, this living witness through whom the light of the spirit of wisdom is to be given, will prove that through the senses we are to become intelligently conversant with all the forces in nature. When these five senses are illuminated with the spirit of understanding, there will be no conflict between the natural spirit and the Holy Spirit. Thus the *seventh* sense becomes the soul life and light which lights up the temple of our God—the physical body. The sixth sense, that is the *intuitive*, the Spirit of truth, the Saviour, now restores you to the Father.

His kingdom is come, His will is done in you on the Earth as in Heaven. This life on Earth is the beginning of one Eternal life in the Lord. It begins here and may attain its full unfoldment here, where the human may become the revealed embodiment of the Divine. This is the pure stream from which, "If a man drinks, he will never thirst. It will be in him a well of living water."

THE PROCREATIVE LAW.

THE Science of Life, known as the laws of God, or the revelation of such, and the identification of the eternal in the temporal, is the object of this work, so as to prove that the laws of the spiritual world are analogous with those of the natural world. Supernatural law is the Great Time-piece wound up, once for all, for every human soul, in its physical as well as spiritual existence, by the great Law Giver, the King of Kings, the Maker of the Law of Laws. which proceeds from the great inorganic central soul pervading the universe, and which reveals itself through every organic body that lives. It is that which gives unity of perfection in all the infinite varieties and complex relations of vital force, by and through which the laws of attraction and repulsion operate, uniting and separating, adding to and taking from, subservient to the laws of involution and evolution. No amount of human logic, nor the present known discoveries in natural science, have been able to comprehend fully the Divine Law and Order of Creation; in its protection and destruction, as it is first spiritually discerned.

Man simply admired the grandeur of Divine Law
and Order in the universe over his head, as also in
the mineral, vegetable and animal kingdoms around
him, but he is perfectly powerless in himself to define what he sees, feels or in any way perceives, unless taught or permitted to learn by the Spirit of
the Divine.

Man's highest intellect must admit that the constant law of motion existing in the greater bodies
is also unceasingly working in the lesser ones; and
that man and woman made in the image and likeness
of the Creator, must necessarily possess all the
spiritual forces to perfection.

That is the ultimate end in view, in the workings of the Divine Mind, through the natural and
spiritual organism of human nature, male and
female. Hence it is through the development of
the soul-nature, that the human mind learns the
perfect workings, of the physical operations in the
functions of the organic laws. This also shows
how the inspiration of the Almighty Mind moves
in the order of Divine harmony; and operates in
and through all laws spiritual and natural. It is
quite essential for man to fully understand himself,
and the impulses of his own nature, before he can
become acquainted with the laws of his own organ-

ism; but this can not be attained through natural study unless you have a Divine Teacher.

This instructor is no less than the spirit of God indwelling with man, the spirit of life, the still small voice, called conscience, the God within which is ever ready to answer to the God without, He, who is the fountain and source of all life, has placed in the human organism, a centre of fixed laws connected with the great centre of inorganic life called God. It is written, "those who know Him and serve Him in spirit are called the sons of God." Jesus hath said, "If ye love me, keep my commandments. And I will pray the Father and He shall give you another Comforter that he may abide with you forever; even the Spirit of truth, whom the world cannot receive because it seeth him not, neither knoweth him, but ye know Him for he dwelleth with you and shall be in you."

Again, "but the Comforter which is the Holy Ghost whom the Father will send in my name, he shall teach you all things and bring all things to your remembrance whatsoever I have said unto you." "And when he is come he will reprove the world of sin and of righteousness and of judgment. Of sin, because they believe not on me; of righteousness because I

go to my Father and ye see me no more ; of judgment because the prince of this world is judged."
" He will guide you into all truth for he shall not
speak of himself but whatever he shall hear, that
shall he speak and he will show you things to
come."

This interior life flows in and out through those
divinely connected in oneness of spirit. This
Divine law is made manifest in procreation ; but it
is in the human form alone that we can find the
governing principles of all law ; that which blends
with all forms of life, yet in itself master and ruler
over all, the harmonizer of all, and the life of all.
Each individual through its connection with the
great life-centre, has power to draw to itself all the
requisite life, force and power that it needs.
Jesus said, " I could ask my Father and He could
send me legions of Angels."

Angels is another name for spiritual life in the
form of an intelligent force, a unity of power
which could have saved Jesus from apparent death
on the Cross, had he so desired to save his natural
life ; but as our example, and true to His mission,
He had to submit His human form to death, so
that He might prove to the world that the inner
law of His being, the spirit of His life could draw

to itself a power by which natural death could be overcome, destroyed. Thus to live after the Law or the leadings of the spirit of Truth, is to be forever with God : but to be carnally minded is to be under the bondage of ignorance, sin and death,—as it is written, " The wages of sin is death"; "but to those who walk after the spirit of life there is no death." "Spirit is life, and the love of the spirit of life in Christ Jesus saves from the law of sin and death."

In the human soul in its organic form we find light and darkness, ignorance and intelligence, also heat and cold, the positive and negative forces. These principles are the same that exist in the heavenly bodies, which revolve in their own orbits, the greater embodying the lesser, each in itself complete. Under the same principle each man is complete in himself, when the Divine law of his being, the inorganic principle is made manifest in the human organism, the corporal body. Thus every individual is threefold in its nature, possessing all that can make one Godlike, also all the possibilities in Nature's Laboratory in its infinitismal form, molucular and animalcular in its excresence embodied in mass, and distributed equally by sympathetic laws, causing man in his attributes to commune with all formation of life either ignorantly or intelligently. Animal life, being the first form of creation, it is the basis on which the human law rests. Animal law is second in degree and thereby subject to the human law. Human reason should therefore rule and regulate animal life in man. When animal life is allowed to rule the human reason, the law is reversed and the human nature becomes lower than that of the beast. This is why there is so much suffering in all the domestic relations of life; sickness, sorrow, degradation, and death follows in succession. Humanity is rioting with this state of unrighteousness, and failing to govern or control it, simply because human reason is not submissive to the Divine will; the fundamental law of our inmost being.

The inorganic principle of the great law of life should rule the animal and the human. This Divine element is the inmost and outermost of man; and where it finds sufficient scope, it bursts forth into a Divine human. This is the perfect law of life, the law of liberty revealing a complete creation, wherein the animal and the human are embodied in the Divine, "I will walk in you and talk in you. I will be your God, and you will be my people." This explains Christ's words also, "I am

in the Father and ye are in me, and I am in you ;
as the branch cannot bear fruit unless it abides in
the vine ; even so, neither can ye, except ye abide
in me."

Christ was the spirit of life in Jesus. How
blessedly He tried to lead men into the knowledge
of the truth as it was revealed in Him. How his
inmost soul-life flowed out to an ignorant and way-
ward people, and with what perfect love to those
who sacrificed all to follow Him, He said, when
praying to the Father for them, " I in them and Thou
in me that they may be made perfect in one."

These words distinctly point to our three fold
nature, the innermost, the outermost, and the intermediate, thus proving that all features are under
one Divine law, and that it is the law of the spirit of
life, which is the motive power in all, and over all.
Life in its Divinity is as varied in its visible and in-
visible forms and expressions, as God himself is
illimitable and immeasurable. Hence the apparent
entire hopelessness of the finite comprehending the
Infinite. But when we know God and acknowledge
him as our life and soul, our Teacher and Saviour,
our constant companion and Revelator, it is only
then, and not until then, that we find, ' there is
nothing in the economy of Providence which our

childlike faith and obedience desires, but what it will receive. "Ask and it will be given," is a Divine promise which has been verified in all ages, and among all nations, when the natural and the spiritual mind have agreed in musical harmony of understanding.

In infancy and childhood, there are spiritual glimpses, visible in all our thoughts, expressions and acts, guileless and spontaneous, which if developed would manifest a fund of spiritual life, in store for us as a provision for the eternal future. But soon in boyhood, and girlhood other natural heart and carnal mind apes the bewildering evil association, and practically smothers the passive growth of spiritual life; yet the soul nature holds it up in trust for the heavenly child of the Great Spirit; until it attains the age and state of ripeness, a change which is tritely called the second birth by our Great Preacher and Teacher Christ the Lord.

Spiritual aspiration is the law of growth. Nothing grows profitably unless the growth is a natural development as well as a spiritual; for example, one may be placed in association with a set of very religious people. The atmosphere of these earnest minds will prevail over that of the novice, and will stimulate an action or operation of the same principle in this individual. At first it may be tedious and monotonous, especially so, if that be the first experience with him in religious thoughts. It is very apt to be confusing until the individual has been brought into harmony with the nature of the same line of thought, manifesting itself in the surrounding minds.

On the same principle that a plant under glass in a hot house, will develop a more rapid growth than if allowed to grow in an open space, where it is exposed to sudden changes of sunshine, shower and frost. In the one we have the cultivated, and in the other we have the natural growth and development, both partaking of the outgrowth of circumstances, still retaining their peculiar faculties and capacities. The life of each springs from the same germ ; yet the one may be perfected in all its spiritual and natural bloom, while the other may be tossed hither and thither by the rude hand of circumstances ; and in the battle for natural life and existence, one may bloom out a hardier and more enduring individual, than the other trained in the nursery of refinement and carefulness. There is danger of ripening into a spiritual understanding without the physical power of expressing what the spirit life is ; as it has been unfolded in these exclusive religious lives.

To know a divine principle or command, and not
to have physical power to express or to live it out
boldly, is an extreme of an incidental umbrage which
will soon fade away like that of an eclipse. The
forced growth and the season charm of an hot house
plant, compared to the stout off-shoots and the ma-
jestic beauty of nature's green house. The strength
and bloom of the forest gives an instructive con-
trast to a student of the law of procreation.

Religion is so much after this manner that we
have both the extremes—one ardent and zealous,
and the other cold and indifferent. When
the cold, calculating mind is warmed up by the
fire of truth, it is very apt to go to the other extreme;
here, again, is the balance lost at least for a time.
Indeed, for some the opportunity is lost until found
in the footsteps of eternity. These religious extremes cause a lack of natural balance, which
lowers the value of all good said or done, as the
incompleteness of the truth, given in part, lacks the
roundness of the whole.

God is perfect, and Jesus told His disciples " to
be perfect even as their Heavenly Father was perfect." When the spirit and the principles of the
laws of God, are lived out by those who profess to
be followers of the meek and lowly Jesus, they will

then understand the word of the law, also the love
and the life which manifests through all law. Law
is order. When the spirit of true religion is lived
out in human souls, there will be no confusion. There
will be no inharmony, between the mind of man and
the members of the man's body. Each man, then,
will have become a law unto himself or herself. All
will know God, from the youngest to the oldest.
Religion and science have before them a great work
to do for each other. One cannot say to the other,
I need thee not. One cannot attain perfection
without the other. It is time they join hands, so
that they may walk together in the path of knowledge of the law and order of God, natural as well
as spiritual, where no two can walk in, unless in
complete agreement. .

Herein lies the need of union among men, so as
to have the spirit of harmony set up on this earth,
that the laws of life may be wisely unfolded, and
taught understandingly to all, that a developed
people in God may be the outgrowth of the generations of many who have come and gone, and yet stay
here earth-bound waiting for the day of deliverance,
"the day of light which is to enlighten every man
that cometh into this world." The torchlight of the
so-called Goddess of Liberty, is only a beacon

for those living within a circumscribed area; but
the everlasting sunshine of the day of deliverance, marks the path of the dead, as well as of
the living, the just and unjust. Jesus lived the laws of
God and became greater than the law, for it is only
through living the laws that the love and wisdom of
all laws are made manifest to us, and through us to
others. This knowledge gives the power to live the
law that works by love; and love is the fulfilling of
the law. This is why the miracles of Jesus confused
and confounded those who lived under the law and
who were only trying to keep the law, yet under
bondage to ignorance of the right knowledge of the
law, they held the law of love subject to their knowledge of law. But the Christ in Jesus convinced
and convicted many a mighty wiseacre of that day,
and is doing the same down to this, our day, through
his words and manifested power, proving that the
law which works by love takes captivity captive and
gives gifts unto men.

The gift of health, the gifts of spiritual sight, and
spiritual understanding; the wealth of love and the
power to keep the laws of our God, as revealed in
Christ Jesus, also to be revealed in all who take up
their cross and follow in his footsteps; these live in
the promise, they shall walk in the light as He

walked in the light, and they shall have fellowship one with another," for the blood of Jesus Christ cleanseth us from all sin. Here let me say the word blood causes many persons to stumble, but that is not meant the fluid that flowed from His wounds on the cross, it is the profuseness of the spirit that flowed through all his words and acts. The love of the Father when understood was the spirit and power of the life of Jesus. He gave life to all that came to Him. He was life to all who needed life, the very spirit of His word gave life, physical life. His natural life was a substituting life for both natural and spiritual, and to all who received Him, to them He gave power to become the sons of God. He gave them of His own life. He was in the will and knowledge of the Father, and His divine mission as a teacher made Him a Saviour to all who would learn of Him. In fact he lived for the Father and not for Himself, swallowing the bitterest cup with these words, "not as I will, but as Thou wilt."

These principles of total surrender He left with His disciples, promising that all who believed and acted up to His word, even through them, He would manifest Himself, and they would be "bone of His bone and flesh of His flesh."

Here, again, we are called to the law where all are equal, where there is only one spirit and there is only one class of material matter through which the same spirit of life reveals itself. There are many operations and demonstrations of the same spirit, but only one Lord over all. In the human we have the animal life in the form of male and female as the highest type of material creation. Man, male and female, is mentally and physically endowed with the capability of development, by which the animal nature may become the revealed human, the earthly dwelling place of the divine. Man as an animal may only develope his animal nature, and through a cultivated intellect he may attain to great natural and physical endowments, also the knowledge of good and evil giving him the capability of ruling as a man, over other men, under certain humane and moral considerations, but as we have said before, he is only an educated animal, whether he be male or female, unless the spirit of the divine nature is quickened in him.

The interior law of being which unites spirit, soul and body together. This is the law of the three in one which makes the complete man and woman. The divine spirit unites body and soul together, and shines forth like a wedding garment,

covering our body and soul with love and wisdom.
This is the mantle of charity which Jesus Christ
covered His people with. " By grace are ye saved,
and not by any means of yourselves, lest ye should
boast." As the body and soul has no vital force or
power but what comes from the interior life, hence
neither the body nor the soul can boast of its own
self-endorsement, without robbing God, or in other
words, robbing self, as the spirit is the seat of life,
it is the real personality to whom all honor is due.
This three-fold nature has been so mystified that
the key to Christ's religion, given as a revelation of
the laws of Moses, has become, in the hands of intellectual minds, a barrier rather than a help to
those who are seeking light, or the knowledge of
the way of salvation.

Religion should be a living fire, through which all
our acts, words and thoughts must pass, and stand
proof of the divine love in the individual soul; this
principle of love has been kept alive all through the
ages. God has never left Himself without a witness
among even the worst class of people and in the
darkest times. Abel, Noah, Abraham, Isaiah, Jere-
miah, Job, Daniel and innumerable others have
shone in the partial bloom of divine love, and
testified as lights for the good of humanity.

Man has, through his intellectual perception of God's word, drawn deductions therefrom, which he has classified and promulgated to the great detriment of pure religion. Man has set himself up as a teacher, when he is living himself on the animal plane, not having attained to the divine power of self-government, which is the only standard whereby a man is called of God ; and sent forth as a teacher of others. No man, however well informed he may be, if he has not overcome the power of breaking the law himself, he cannot possibly teach others how to keep it ; as it is written, " how can you teach, or preach, except ye be sent of God." Men are teaching religion who are not in their own nature able to keep the law. The blind are leading the blind. Men are governing through their intelligent animal or human conception of the laws, hence discords abound, wars and hostilities have been and are still the prevailing order of the natural minds.

Religious preaching, as a business, has been enlisted in the same category with the works of the hammer and the hand. Theological workshops are opened for the beating of brains, to fit them to handle the materials from the pew to the pulpit. The elasticity of the steel thus hammered does not last for more than twenty-four hours, nor does it extend beyond the compound of the houses set apart for religious performances.

Human intellect has found that laboring in the sacred cause on the first day, pays well for a rest of the following six days, and this mania has taken possession of the brightest intellects, so that the inherent spiritual light has been totally eclipsed; by the natural and human attempts of making most of everything, that meets the material wants of the body physical. Spiritual hunger and spiritual thirst is nowhere quenched; nay, even the natural is hardly overcome.

Science is taught from the same standard. Men through their intellectual ambition try to find out God and his works, through searching the astronomical bodies. Geologians sink deep in the bowels of the earth, to read in the streaks of the different strata if possible, the agencies recorded through the footprints of time. Here we find a school of minds, some in astronomy, and others in meteorology, all trying to find, in natural philosophy, the evidences of God's laws; yet none have found God himself.

To find Him one has only to look within themselves; there we hear the still small voice which says in audible tones, "come, let us reason together."

Herein we find the spirit of our creator saying to the spirit of the natural man, "be still and know that I am God."

When the outer and intermediate life of the human soul is still; the inner life, the spring of the eternal law of God will make itself, intelligently felt and heard.

This is the word of God verified in the saying, "God is in His holy temple, let the earth keep still." Man and woman look at each other and pattern after each other, instead of listening to the inner guide, the God of each household; individualized in himself. All good expressed by others find a response in our soul when we are in consultation with our God, our inner guide.

Thus we are enabled to approve and disapprove and thereby learn of Him who was meek and lowly, and thus become strengthened through the example of good in others. But when we try to follow in the light of the good works of others, we are only observers of truth; enjoying the good that others do is only warming ourselves by another's fire. Unless you are living the truth which you see and hear you are only a hearer of the word, not a doer. Hence your life is the reflex action of other lives, consequently you are unfruitful, like the fig tree.

DUO-DECIMAL PRINCIPLE IN CREATION.

The twelve Constellations, or as they are known the twelve signs of the Zodiac, signify or represent the systematic twelve principles in Creation; divided first by the twelve hours of day and the twelve hours of night. These twenty-four hours make a cycle of measurement indicating the time of a rotary motion, in which the Earth revolves on her axis in conjunction with the Sun. The Moon's time is calculated by months instead of by Day and Night. Her increasing and decreasing phases, making twelve times twelve which mark a cycle of time out of which will be gathered together the twelve thousand times twelve thousand perfect souls from the twelve tribes of Israel. Hence man and woman are principled in the Sun, Moon and Stars, but first developed in the order of Day and Night, having in themselves individually, light and darkness, heat and cold, positive and negative forces, acting and acted upon from and to all points of the compass, from the uppermost point of the zenith, to the lowermost point of the nadir;

known as the Electric and Magnetic currents. The
relative laws of attraction and repulsion. When
these and other laws are understood as practically
working in and through the human body, there will
be complete harmomy between the planetary systems and the human race, proving, therefore, that
nature does not destroy itself. It approves and dis-
approves by the law of attraction and repulsion ; yet
it is connected harmoniously by the love principle,
known as the spirit of the law of Involution and
Evolution. When these laws are known to man in
spirit, all things will be in common, as in the early
Apostolic Church.

The pnenomena in nature as well as in spirit will
be an open book, distinctly showing the common
working of both the p hysical and spiritual nature of man on earth, and in the planetary systems.
Now the law of attraction is the only one that men
and women wish to recognise in each other as it
communicates sympathetically according to the gravitation of their natural and spiritual life. The law of
repulsion similarly repels, bringing forth strife and
warfare between individuals, and causes them to fly
apart or clash against each other on the principle that
no two can walk together unless agreed. These
centripetal and centrifugal forces are natural in the

human development, and also visible in the elementary world between the earth and the suns, which rule the earth and the heavenly bodies.

As yet there has been no one save Jesus who understood the law of repulsion. He gave to it the right of way, as the law of repulsion, or he rebuked it, and in love overcame it. His followers will, without contention, overcome by the characteristic and sublime gift of His reasoning spirit, " the seed and root of their spiritual growth in wisdom and love." Man and woman naturally want to attract each other, and that which detracts from them they consider their enemy. Thus attraction or love is spontaneous and spiritual, while detraction or enmity is artificial and carnal. The first has its self-existence, while the second is often the product of circumstances. The law of cause and effect is naturally understood as want and supply. This is carnal instinct, which belongs to the brute creation. The law of universal sympathy is love and harmony. This is self-existent in men below as in the planets above.

Thus individual selfishness is the result of human gratification, educational surroundings, and is, after all, a momentary happiness absorbed by an individual from those who are made negative in proportion

to their selfish power over them. This positive
element of selfish character in a man or woman is
visible in the domestic tyrant, or one who puts
forth might over right, that lives like a parasite on
the life-blood of others.   "Love is life;" it is
order—"Heaven's first law."

Nature has given to each month in the year its
own order of time and its effect.   The subdivision
of months into days, hours, moments and seconds
has each its share of duty in this grand march of
Time. One does not vie with the other—no clash,
no gap, no vacuum.   There is nothing in the order
of the Heavens but harmony, union and succession, all linked together, encompassing the whole
sphere of Creation.   In this law of harmony we are
able to see the providences of Divine order in the pe-
riodical visitations of storms and earthquakes,
their special missions.   In them the law of attraction and repulsion is the means by which our earth's .
atmosphere is purified. Were it not for the sunshine and the shower, also the winds and the thunder and lightnings, the whirlwinds and the whirl-
pools, we would have been unable to breathe the
poisonous air arising from the inharmony of earth's
mixed elements, their strifes, contentions, and
emanations, ascending and descending gaseous va-
pors.

The Great Lawmaker has blessedly provided space between the firmament of the heavens and that of the earth for the display of these forces, the battle ground of these destructive elements. He has also placed beyond the reach of man the self-regulated suns and moons, with their attractive and repulsive forces, so that man's intellectual and animal nature cannot interfere with the Divine law of motion.

Man has tried to read the signs in the heavens, and has also tried to navigate the air. In both instances he has had a measure of success, but until man first becomes reconciled to himself and his Creator, subject to all the laws of his own being as affected by the gravitation, attraction and repulsion of his surroundings and circumstances—his environments—he will not know, consequently cannot gain the knowledge of the laws which would enable him to read clearly the firmament of the heavens and perceive the workings of all laws. The promise of God is to him who overcometh. Hence it is given to the overcomer to say to the winds and to the waves, as Jesus did, "Be still," and they obeyed Him, and to the sun, as Joshua commanded, and the sun stood still.

Man, although made in the image of his Creator,

is to-day very far from the love and wisdom principles which harmonize and understandingly rule in
oneness of spirit with the Divine. Sad it is, yet
true, that the conforming principles of the procreative law of life is an enigma to man; still, as man
corresponds to all the laws of life in the heavenly,
in addition to his knowledge of the laws of life in
the earthly, he must attain to the summit of his
power, as he is created in the image and likeness of
God. But now he is unwisely searching through
the three kingdoms—mineral, vegetable and animal
—for the anatomy of nature in all its varied phases,
for the knowledge of truth which is contained and
buried in his own soul.

The intellectual man is hunting after the secret
outside of himself, like the musk-deer that smells
the substance he himself produces, and yet not
knowing where it is lodged, runs after it from hill to
hill and valley to valley. Man is more ignorant
than that animal of instinct. The animal runs for
its own sake, while man strives that he may be considered great by mortals. With such a selfish
motive for attaining human glory, it is no wonder
that man has entirely failed to find the pearl of
great price.

Greatness and goodness is to be found in its only

place—the spirit, the inner self which giveth life, love and truth to all for the good of all. When this spirit which is given to all, blooms out in each of us individually, the love and wisdom of the Infinite mind will make us consciously and intelligently part and parcel of itself, also a part of the whole universal creations. When the mental illumination of God's spirit shows itself in you and in me, dear reader, it will be the revealed mind of Christ; and Christ is God. Here then is the original principle of life given in the procreative law blooming out in the likeness of its Creator, the Christ.

The fruits of such a life is peace and joy, love and wisdom. This gives us the verified promise, that as Jesus was in this world so shall we be. Jesus wisely said He was with the Father from the beginning. His Father and our Father, the Creator, has never changed his laws. They are from the beginning; they have no end, as they begin in Him and end in Him. He is omnipresent and omnipotent. The Alpha and Omega, who gave life to the world and the very law of that life, brings to perfection from the seed or germ a perfect life, and when perfected it is like Him. It is Him.

The child and the parent are one in spirit, in one eternal understanding, as there is only one God;

and although there are many children, there is only one spirit in all, the universal spirit of law and order, whose basis is love and wisdom.

DAY AND NIGHT—THE TWENTY-FOUR HOUR SYSTEM

The law of procreation places man first in the order of earth's creations under the twenty-four hour system of Day and Night. This brings him, by the laws of attraction and repulsion, subject to the elements of discords in the earth's vegetating, undeveloped and decomposed state. This order of life, in its undeveloped condition, gives us one great mass of human souls born after the law of procreation, yet conceived in lust; thereby we are propagating the animal side of life in each one thus born, which rules and robs the spiritual of its true place, its birthright, thus proving the Scripture, "That those born after the flesh persecute those born after the spirit." But this order of natural rule passes away through the quickening knowledge and new births of the spirit. Truly, Mother Nature is under the yoke of bondage, the slave of natural propensities, represented as woman in chains. Surely woman is chained to her own hereditary conditions through the masculine mind she affiliates with. Thus the children are the representatives of these parental conditions.

Need we wonder, then, at the grossness of the destructive elements of these ante-natal conditions as they appear, and are known as the battle of Christ and Antichrist. Antichrist is the animal, or self-love, rebelling against the spirit, ignorantly and understandingly.

THE LIGHT OF THE SUN AND MOON.

The light of the moon by night represents the earth's children in their undeveloped spiritual approximation to spiritual intelligence. The moon's monthly appearances, from the time she changes until she arrives at her full circle of light, are symbolic of the finite mind in its gradual growth, fullness and decline.

This moon-mother represents also, in the twelve hours of night, that the finite mind, while under bondage to sin and the sins of ignorance, has only a partial light, and therefore is incapable of walking in the full light of day. Jesus said, "Those who walk in the day do not stumble," meaning the full understanding of their relation to God. For example, the sun gives light by day, and his attractive power of light and heat is the motor, which keeps the earth in motion. The moon is called the natural governor, the earth-mother, to whom the undeveloped offspring of earth goes, as it is written, "When the father and mother forsake their child, the Lord takes it up."

The moon's power over the tides and temperature is all due to the influences of other heavenly bodies upon the moon. Many are affected pleasantly and unpleasantly by her light. The twelve signs of the Zodiac influence us all, more or less, through the moon.

THE DIVINE LAW OF MOTION.

The twelve constellations are the revolving principles by which the earth and the heavens are held in place. Around the Zodiac everything in heaven above and on the earth beneath are in limitation to these principles, and are as outlets of this central circle of suns, each one holding its law of attraction and repulsion in its gravitating power to and from the earth, touching each individual sphere on the earth. Herein lies the mystery of the laws of creation and procreation, also the order and line of growth of each earthly parent

tree, the origin and genealogies of each tribe recorded.   The twelve tribes of Israel are here represented in the Zodiac, the Astral book of life,
which keeps the record of all human life.

Each human soul holds its own individuality
intact in this Astral record, yet is only representing
a branch of the first order of creation.   Thus, in
the circle of twelve, we have in each human soul
the twelve principles of Divine order in the unity
of oneness.   When woman is freed from the
chains of earthly bondage, walking in the spiritual
light and freedom of her soul nature, she will
stand, in the knowledge of all these life principles,
" clothed with the sun, and the moon under her feet."

THE GENESIS OF LIFE.

WE hope to show the relation of the natural senses to those of the spirit; also the physical body and its relation to the brain; also the relation of the natural man to the Solar system, the Astral Heavens; also the creative forces which exist between individuals and the general order of life, by which each and all revolve in their own order, complete in themselves, yet each a part of the perfect working of the whole. Man in his relative attributes has the twelve principles of the completeness of the true order of creation in himself. "In the beginning God created the Heavens and the Earth. God said—let there be light, and there was light. And God made the firmament and called the firmament Heaven. And God said let there be lights in the firmament of the Heavens to divide the Day from the Night, and let them be for signs and for seasons and for days and years. And God made two great lights, the greater light to rule the day and the lesser light to rule the night; He made the stars also —and God set them in the firmament

of the Heavens to give light upon the Earth. And
God said let the Earth bring forth grass, the herb
yielding seed and the fruit tree yielding fruit, after
its kind, whose seed is in itself, upon the Earth ; and
the Earth brought forth fruit. And God said let
the waters bring forth abundantly moving creatures
that have life, and fowls that may fly above the
Earth in the open firmament of the Heavens. And
God said let the Earth bring forth the living creatures after its kind —And God said let us make man
in our own image—In the image of God created
he him, male and female created He them. And
God blessed them and said unto them, be fruitful,
multiply and replenish the Earth and subdue it
and have dominion over the fish of the sea and over
the fowls of the air, and over every living thing that
moveth upon the Earth. And God said, Behold, I
have given every herb bearing seed which is upon
the face of the Earth for meat, and it was so—And
God saw every thing which He had made and behold it was good ; and the evening and the morning
were the sixth day. Thus the Heavens and the
Earth were finished ; and on the seventh day God
rested from His work which He had made. And
God blessed the seventh day and sanctified it, because that in it He had rested from all His work
which God created and made."

TWELVE ATTRIBUTES OF GOD IN MAN.

A S we have shown by the creation, we hope
also to prove the corresponding spiritual relation of the God-man, in the firmament of the
heavens, to the earthly man, proving that the Lord's
Prayer, repeated in spirit and in truth, reveals the
will of God done in the human soul in the earthly
body as in the firmament of the heavens. Thus the
heavenly finds its corresponding relation in the
natural man, proving that "it is life eternal to know
Thee, the only true God; and Jesus Christ, whom
Thou hast sent."

ARIES—THE RAM.

In the first constellation, Aries, we find the first
heavenly corresponding likeness to Jesus in the
head and the face of the Ram, or the Lamb, which
is the symbolic sign of Jesus, our Lord and the
Lamb of God.—The meek, gentle and pure Jesus,
who lived the law and attained to the perfect image

and likeness of God, the Creator, and thus became the representative head and face of the Godhead in Aries and in the whole human family on the earth.

Thus the lamblike nature of the God-man in the heavens was in full bloom in the earthly form of Jesus —He whose life proves that if a man subdues and governs the laws of his own nature, he may live in direct correspondence with the laws of the heavenly firmament; hence there is every certainty of all such attaining the same end as the Lamb of God, Jesus the Christ, did.

Beginning with the first sign of the Zodiac, Aries, which the sun enters at the vernal equinox, on the 21st of March, we find that this sign shows our natural sonship in the Great Father, also represents the spiritual sun or sonship that illuminates our mind with the light of love and wisdom, from the natural springtime, through the summer, autumn and winter of our existence. Our inner nature reveals all the beauties of the natural and spiritual sonship and daughterhood, in understanding even to the propagating according to the order of creation—the bringing forth of offspring in due season. Hence, with such knowledge, children would be born in due time; as children born after such a spiritual understanding of the springtime of pure love would be accordingly, in the will of God, and in direct communication with the Divine order of the heavens, and thus occupy their place in the first constellation sign in the heavens, also in the earthly body of man, as taught in the Lord's Prayer, "God's will done in the earth as in Heaven." The purity of infancy is significant of the lamb-like nature, the tender sprouts of the springtime of man and woman's life in God. Hence the offspring is the transmission of this union.

TAURUS—THE BULL.

The second zodiacal constellation has its corresponding place in our earthly body in the neck, significant of man's animal nature, either under the yoke of the spiritual influence of the heavens, as Jesus said, "Take My yoke upon you and learn from Me," or subject to its own instincts and unbridled passions. This animal nature, when domesticated and sanctified, responds to the call of God in man or woman. Each one reveals in his or her face the seal of the spirit, or the predominancy of the animal.

Thus, to a keen observer, each one is labeled, justified, sanctified and glorified, or the opposite of each of these. When the eye is single, the whole body is full of light. Thus, when sealed, we shall represent in our eyes the star Aldebaran, as in the eye of Taurus. Likewise the Hyades, the five stars in our faces, shining out through the five senses, as in the face of Taurus, proving the Scripture, " That the light of the body is the eye ;" thereby showing that, when the five natural senses and the intuitive (the sixth sense) are illuminated, we are in conformity with the spirit of God in the Pleiades, revealing the light of these six stars, signifying the six days of creation in us, the work that God blessed on the seventh, and called it good.

GEMINI—THE TWINS.

Gemini is the third constellation, correspondingly connected with our physical nature in the arms. It contains and represents in us the light of the two bright stars, Castor and Pollox, which, astronomers tell us, give an electrical light often seen at the mast-head and yard-arms of a vessel on a tempestuous night, which when seen portends a cessation of the storm. Here is seen the mariner's guardian angel, the bow of promise, the harbinger of peace. Gemini is our heavenly twin arms, which

carries the electrical storms that our brain, neck
and shoulders often throw off through our arms
and hands.

Yes, the fury of mental storms often spend their
force, for either good or evil, through the natural
arms. All know that the natural man wounds and
sometimes kills with the natural arms and hands;
also heals, soothes and uplifts through these natural members. The writer testifies to the power of
God as a heavenly, golden light, having been seen
and consciously felt by herself, and plainly visible
to others, in her face and flowing from her arms and
hands, when healing the sick, even before she knew
anything of the astronomical signs of the heavens.

We trust that our readers will be able to comprehend their own relationship to Gemini. If they
have not in healing others, they may in the mental
storms of joy and sorrow which have spent their
force through the arms and hands. May we all
remember it is through our arms and hands God
works in and through us in love to the uplifting of
human souls. It is in Gemini that we find the spiritual origin of the laying on of hands. We read in
the Acts, 28th chapter, how St. Paul, after his ship-
wreck, when he was entertained by the barbarians,
and they saw that the viper on his hand hurt him

not, and he healed many of their diseases, that the people said, " He is a God." And he stayed on the island of Melita three months, and sailed from there on a ship of Alexandria whose sign was Castor and Pollox.

Astronomy tells us that the sun enters the third constellation sign, Gemini, about the 25th of May. We read that May was called the Pentecostal month in the early Apostolic days. It was their fruit time and harvest. The Hebrews called it the Feast of Weeks, because it was kept seven weeks after the Passover. Hence the 6th of May has been considered the Festival of Thanksgiving by the Hebrews for the ingathering of the harvest; also in commemoration of being delivered from Egyptian servitude. It is said by good authority that the very day of Pentecost was the same day on which God delivered the Law from Mount Sinai; (Ex., XIX, 11), and likewise the day the Apostles were filled with the Holy Spirit. Quotations from the Scripture: Acts, II, 1.—"When the day of Pentecost was fully come." Acts, II, 16.—" He hastened to be at Jerusalem on the day of Pentecost." I Cor., XVI, 8.—"But I will tarry at Ephesus until Pentecost."

All this proves that in those days there was an

observance of this sign in the heavens. Although I find no time when the relation of the physical nature to that of the spiritual was in full and perfect understanding, save in Christ Jesus' nature, the spiritual man has always been in harmony with himself, but imperfectly understood by the natural man; still at certain times, such as this Pentecostal season, when the sun enters the constellation Gemini, the people prayed, praised, fasted and feasted, and received on both soul and body the outpourings of the Holy Spirit. This is an evidence that there are times and seasons when we can and do receive more spiritual blessings than at other times. To me, dear reader, it was the fullness of time—the 6th of May—the harvesting time of my spiritual and bodily resurrection.

On May the 5th, 1871, at 10 A. M., I passed away; that is, I gave myself away to God and believed myself dying, and for twenty-six hours I lay as one dead, with mourning friends around me, and attended by four physicians, who believed me to be in that state called death. Yet I was spiritually alive, hearing all that was said, knowing all that was done, however unable to give physical sign of life, until 12 o'clock on the 6th of May. Thus to me the 6th of May was the resurrection and the judgment, and the Pentecostal endowment of power, which has been with me ever since as my natural and spiritual life, my soul-light and delight, and ever will be, in a world without end.

CANCER—THE CRAB.

Having shown the relation of the head, neck and arms of man to the first three signs of the Zodiac, we will take up the fourth sign, Cancer, located correspondingly in the human breast. The breast of man is his lungs and chest. The sign, Cancer, represents the Summer Solstice. It gives to man and woman the holy and celestial influences of the summer land, which always keeps the breast and bosom of man and woman full of life, love, tenderness and sunshine.

If the natural man and woman will only abide in their true relation to God, they will always have a heavenly communing with the constellation sign, Cancer. But if they do not abide in the spiritual relationship, they will have the elements of Capricorn, the Winter Solstice, which makes a person cold, capricious and often full of cancerous humors that affect the human soul and body, from the slight eruption on the skin to the virulent tumors consum-

ing the flesh in various ways, until death releases
the imprisoned soul. True, there is deliverance from
these conditions and diseases without going out of
the body to get it. It is in dying to self, and turn-
ing away from all these evils or ills of the flesh to
God, who is your life. Then, as it is promised,
"none of these diseases will have power over you,
for I am the God who healeth all thy diseases and
forgiveth all thy offences." God our Father is the
spirit sign in Cancer—the Holy Spirit, the Earthly
Governor, "Christ in you the hope of glory."

LEO—THE LION.

Leo, the Lion, the fifth sign in the Zodiac, represents the fifth principle in the heavenly, which corresponds to the Divine earthly in the human heart.
This is the star of Hope in every human soul, that
leadeth the mind upward and onward as truly as
the needle points correctly in the compass, guiding
the mariner's course. So surely will this star
guide each one of us, as it did the wise men of the
East, to the Heavenly Leo—the Christ-child—called
in the Holy Writ the Lion of the Tribe of Judah.

The true natural representative of the fifth constellation is Jesus Christ, the Righteous. He who

was sent of the Father to bind up the broken-hearted and to open the prison doors of those that were bound ; who said, "Blessed are the pure in heart, for they shall see God," and those that call on the Lord out of a pure heart; those that love one another with a pure heart; all that believed were of one heart. "Those who seek me with the whole heart shall find me." The heart is the heavenly seat of pure love, courage and understanding, likewise grief and pleasure. We read of "a broken heart," "a clean heart," "an evil heart," "a hardened heart," "a liberal heart, a heart that does an act of kindness freely, voluntarily and with generosity."

Jesus summed up the law of God thus: "To love God with all your heart, soul, mind and strength, and love thy neighbor as thyself is the whole law." This is the Gospel of God. No man can do more than this—to lay down his life for another; and to be able to do this is to have the kingdom of God within you. Leo, the Lion sign in the heavens, would then be revealed in the man earthly, shining forth in his life. When this true relation exists between man and his God, "the lion and the lamb will lie down together, and none will make them afraid."

VIRGO—THE VIRGIN.

Virgo, the Virgin, is the next sign in order, the sixth constellation, having, like the former signs, its counterpart or corresponding relations manifested in the human form. Virgo, or Virgin, is located in the bowels, extending to the kidneys, or reins Here we find the seat of life in man and woman, also the union of the Virgin mother, Virgo, with Libra (the seventh constellation), the king of justice.

The great lawmakers, Virgo and Libra, hold unitedly the central office of all law. Out of this human central office flows all lines of gravitation, either upward or downward. This is the central office from which man and woman ascend spiritually and descend.

Astronomers tell us that Virgo now occupies chiefly the sign Libra and contains the bright star Spica. This star of the first magnitude shines forth as the governor of law and order in the heavens, representing the Goddess of Liberty, the Virgin power; corresponding also to the opening of the Third Seal, the three-fold nature of man and woman perfected; Justice holding the balances, crying out, "A measure of wheat for a penny, and three measures of barley for a penny, and see that thou touch not the oil and the wine."

As Virgo, or Virgin, now occupies chiefly the sign Libra, we have, by the light of Divinity, discovered the lost sciences: (the secret of virgin power as it existed in the heavens above, and as it assumed the virgin seat of life in the human soul below, in the beginning of creation.) Webster defines the word virgin as a "female of unspotted purity;" "she who has had no carnal knowledge of man;" "a person of the male sex who is perfectly chaste, who has not known sexual indulgence." "These are they which were not defiled with woman, for they were virgins."—Rev., XIV, 4.

The virgin seat of life takes us back to the creation, when God said, "Let us make man in our own image;" for as the law of life was in the beginning, so it is, and ever will be to the end of the world. God is infinite. His laws are unchangeable. His spirit is not progressive. It is the perfect principle of life in each soul; the spirit of truth which holds the balance of power for good in every human being who is centered in the sign of Virgo; the still, small voice of God; the law of conscience, which works in the soul and mind as the Revelator and Regenerator and brings into human perfection a perfected individual soul, a Christ life, a Divine human, through whom the light of Divinity will shine in correspondence with the twelve constellations in the heavens.

From these luminaries the whole heavens derive not alone their light, but equilibrium, the equalization of the whole; yet every one of the twelve constellations holds its own place in the order of the heavens, the power of each being equal and universal as a whole. In like manner there are twelve personalities in every well-formed human brain, which have to be regulated and harmonized, one to the other, that each may sustain itself in its natural and spiritual order, its earthly and heavenly relationships. Thus the earthly body and mind has to be properly unfolded and wisely developed, so as to receive and hold its heavenly corresponding proportions.

A man or woman perfected belongs to the planetary system as fully as they do in the human order of God on the earth. This knowledge comes to us through Virgo, the Virgin, and Libra, he who holds the balances.

LIBRA—THE BALANCE.

The seventh constellation, the seventh sign in

the heavens, representing the seven days of creation; also the seven senses—seeing, hearing, smelling, tasteing, feeling, thinking and speaking. These
are the seven attributes of God in man and woman.
These are the seven eyes which looked out of the
stone placed before Joshua (Zac., III, 5). These
are the seven angels of the heavens and the seven
seals which only the Lion of the Tribe of Judah
could open. "He alone was found worthy to open
the book." As it is written, "None know the
Father save the Son, and those to whom the Son
reveals Him."

We have also the seven sisters in the Pleiades, six
of whom remained virgins, and are now waiting for
the return of the first virgin daughter of the seventh
sister, the one who wedded Mortality. This virgin-
mother cannot become a virgin in her original bril-
liancy, until an earthly daughter of hers has attained
to the purity of perfected understanding, which is
Christ in woman. This attainment in one of earth's
daughter's closes the cycle of time, revealing the
Deity, or the Divinity in the form of woman. This
is the natural woman," clothed with the sun, and the
moon under her feet," spoken of in Revelations.

Through this Christ-Woman the satellites will be
entranced, or eclipsed, and out of this entrancement

woman rises from her Egyptian darkness into the light of her destined place, where the virgin-mother stood in her first estate, before she went forth as the spiritual seed of life, the one to whom the Infinite God spoke when He said, "Let us make man in our own image, male and female."

Daughters of Zion, when this fullness of time has come, it will give to the daughters of man their new moons and Sabbaths for the restoration and regeneration of new forms and forces on the earth, in the air, and in the planetary systems of the universe of worlds. Then the Seen and the Unseen will walk hand in hand together, brother will greet brother in spirit and in truth, sisters and mothers will be in consort with the armies of the heavenly host, conquering and to conquer. For the seven sisters are again united, and through this earth-union of the one sister who left Heaven to give life to earthly form, and whose life has been revealed in one of her daughters, she is again one with those who are celestial lights, fixed stars in the firmament of the heavens.

This seventh sister of the Pleiades is the mother of all living. She resurrected her Son Jesus, the Christ, nearly nineteen hundred years ago. He was the Redeemed Son, the first-born of many generations. He was the Redeemer in man. He left the human love for the Heavenly, that he might become a vessel of honor, a human soul filled with Divine love towards a darkened, sinful world. He was the revealed life of Divine humanity. He was the perfect, the God-man. Thus man cannot err who follows in his footsteps. He is the perfect model to pattern after; yet since his day we have had no one just like him. No other Christ-man. Why is this? Dear reader, I am told it is because the ages are waiting for the Revelation of the seventh sister and the first earthly perfected daughter of God and of man. She, like Jesus the Christ, has left the world to serve her God, and thereby has become a vessel of honor, in and through whom the sons and daughters of earth may receive love, mercy and truth.

The spirit of this Christ-woman, in whom the Holy Catholic Spirit of universal Godliness dwells, will flow in and through all domains of the eternal principles of God, in the organic and inorganic worlds in space. This enlightened state of woman makes her the virgin daughter of God, the so-called bride of Christ, the evening and morning star, the effeminate nature of God. She is, consequently, in her dual nature, wisdom and love to man. She is the

mother, the Jerusalem which has been bound, but
is now free through the descent of the Holy Ghost
—the Jerusalem which is above—the deliverer of
God's people from sin and ignorance. Some may
consider this statement rather mythical, but we find
its corresponding truth in the thirty-eighth chapter
of Job.

God speaks to-day to the intelligent minds of men
and women as He did to Job, when Job was rebelling in his self-righteousness and knowledge. God
said to him "Where wast thou when I laid the
foundations of the earth? Declare, if thou hast understanding, who hast laid the measures thereof,
if thou knowest? or who hath stretched the line upon it? Wherefore art the foundations thereof fasten-
ed? or who laid the corner stone thereof, when the
morning stars sang together, and all the sons of God
shouted for joy? Canst thou bind the sweet influences of Pleiades or loose the bands of Orion?
Canst thou bring forth Mazzaroth in his season,
(In Hebrew Cimah the seven stars), or canst thou
guide Arcturus with his sons? (In Hebrew Cesil
the twelve signs of the Zodiac?) Knowest thou the
ordinances of heaven? Canst thou set the dominion thereof in the earth? Canst thou lift up
thy voice to the clouds that abundance of waters
may cover thee?"

The whole book of Job sets forth man living in his natural and moral self-righteousness. But this righteousness alone can not answer God to-day any more than in the days of Job. But when Job humbled himself before God, his spirit was united to the spirit of his Creator.

When Job had all his human knowledge swallowed up in the Divine, his prayers for his friends were heard and answered; then God gave back to him twice as much as he had lost. I question, my friends, whether our moral and self-righteous men of to-day, would bear patiently the loss of family and prosperity, to say nothing of bearing the boils and diseases of the flesh, any better than Job; and certianly they know no more of the sweet influences of the Pleiades or the firmament of Heaven than Job did. Therefore they must agree with me, that the flesh profiteth nothing; it is the spirit that giveth life and understanding.

SCORPIO—THE SCORPION.

This brings us to Scorpio, the eighth Constellation sign in the Zodiac, corresponding to the secrets in man and woman. This is the vital principle in the law and order of Procreation, the conjunction and union of two lives in one.   The Divine Word is, "whom *God* hath joined together, let no man put asunder."   This is the spiritual union. The marriage relation of the present day may be likened to the 17th Chapter of Revelations, the marriage contract of the flesh, the judgement of the great whore, called Babylon, the great, the mother of harlots and abominations of the earth, that has made the inhabitants of the earth drunk with the wine of her fornications.

The angel said to John the Revelator, "and I saw the woman drunken with the blood of the saints and with the blood of the martyrs of Jesus."   And the angel further said, "Wherefore didst thou marvel? I will tell thee the mystery of the woman and of the beast that carrieth her, which hath seven heads and ten horns; the beast that thou sawest was and is not, and shall ascend from out of the bottomless pit and go into perdition; and they that dwell on the earth shall wonder, whose names are not written in the Book of Life from the foundation of the world, when they behold the beast that was, and is not, and yet is."

And here is the mind which hath wisdom.   The seven heads are seven mountains on which the woman sitteth, and there are seven kings, five of whom are fallen, and one is, and the other is not yet come. And when he cometh, he must continue a short space of time; and the beast that was and is not, even he is the eighth, and is of the seven, and goeth into perdition." "Here then is wisdom." The seven heads which are spoken of are the seven senses. These are the natural kings. The five natural senses have fallen under the power of the beast, and so has the sixth sense, the intuitive ; it is the king which is, and yet is not, simply because the natural man and woman do not fully realize the sixth sense. They know that there is an inner voice in themselves; but they cannot tell from whence it cometh and whither it goeth, as the beast, or carnal nature, rules this still, small voice of God in the soul. The seventh sense, the king spoken of as not yet come, is speech. The speech of the people is under the beast. This beastly power suppresses the truth; God being the spirit of truth. So, when the seven natural senses are all subject to the spirit of truth, the time of the beast will be short, for the glory of God will be manifested in the people, and the beast will be overcome.

We see that in the past and largely in the present, the seven senses have given their powers to the beast, and now the powers of the eighth (Scor

pio) goeth into perdition, and will carry with it the
natural lusts of the flesh, also the errors and the
evils of the human nature. This reveals to us that
all the natural constellation signs in man and woman
are subject to the beast, unless the human soul is
born again, born of the spirit. At present these
beastly human powers are making war with the
Lamb, and the Lamb of God shall overcome them,
for He is the Lord of Lords and King of Kings,
and they that are with Him are called the chosen
and faithful.—Rev., XVII.

This scripture proves that when Christ is the head
of the man, every member of the body obeyeth the
head [Aries] which is Christ the Lord. Such have
nothing to fear from the beast power, nor from
those born after the flesh. The Scripture clearly
marks the time in which we live. Truly "the sins
of the parents are visited on the children to the
fourth generation." The diseases of inbred and ac-
quired sins are plague spots on the souls
and bodies of the people of every land. The natural sign in the secrets, Scorpio, has not had the
heavenly constellation seal, or the sign of the beast
would not be so visibly seen in the hands and foreheads of the children of men. Yet we are told that
away back in the past, the Lord told Elijah he had

seven thousand who had not bowed the knee to Baal; and there are the hundred and forty and four thousand which John saw, "who came up through great tribulation, and had washed their robes and made them white in the blood of the Lamb."

This is the revealed spirit of Aries in whom the law and love are united. The first sign of the heavenly God-head revealed in human form; who sets in order the household of God, the natural body, the temple, the house not made with hands, eternal in the heavens. But the carnal man only desires his wants supplied, that gratification of the flesh which enables him to attain his human aims and objects.

This he welcomes, whether it be from good or evil; hence he is subject to both worlds. This mortal life is all one life whether mortals are in or out of the body, as mortal spirits of the spirit world are living in and communicating their ideas through the sixth and seventh senses of those in the body. These senses should be the gate of Heaven in the human soul; instead of this they are made the open door to either good or evil influences from the natural and the spirit world.

This is spiritualism, or materialization of spirits called obsession or possession. It is human thought to-day which is flooding the minds, souls and bodies of the people of every land, save those who are born of the spirit and live consciously in open communion with the Holy Spirit.

We are told to beware of seducing spirits, for there is only one God, and He is the God of the living and not of the dead.

Those who live in His will are alive forevermore, and those who live in their own will or that of mortal spirits are dead in trespasses and sins. Consequently, until we are made alive in Christ we are under the beast power, and according to our lives bear the mark of the beast; but when we have died to our own will and have passed from death unto life, then we know Him, whom to know is life; then the seal of the Lamb of God, the Spirit of truth, will be in our foreheads, showing that the power of the beast is overcome in us, and that we belong to the one hundred and forty and four thousand which John saw. Therefore, there is no end to the growth of that soul in grace and in the knowledge of the truth, until it attains manhood and womanhood in the image and likeness of the Creator.

In the knowledge and perfection of the God-head, when the human soul attains to this, the twelve constellation signs will be understood, as the twelve chronometers which keep the order of the Heavens. They are the twelve Angels who keep the twelve gates, to open and close to those who come representing the twelve tribes of Israel. Thus the human soul, born of the spirit, has these twelve representative angels guarding the twelve principles of God, in their natural and spiritual nature corresponding with the angels of the Heavens.

And when the natural is regenerated the dual life is in harmony with the twenty-four hours of day and night, corresponding to the twenty-four elders seen by St. John. Thus "The soul born of God keepeth himself." "He can not sin, because he is born of God." This makes the natural man or woman when born of the spirit, God's house, His tabernacle. "Know ye not that your body is the temple of God; and that the spirit of God dwelleth in you, and the evil one toucheth you not?" Meaning that the evil of the flesh hath no power over you, so as to take you out of the hands of the living God.

This is the revealed nature of Jesus, the Divine human, and as Jesus was in this world, so will you and I be, dear reader, if we are begotten of God. Hence we see the two witnesses in the Heavens and in the Earth, the pure spiritual life of God, male and female, son and daughter, as in the procreative law, a dual life and a perfected soul.

This is the ultimate of the law of the spirit which contains both natures; but owing to the human ignorance of the laws of our being, the natural in the parents predominates over the spiritual, and as it is in the parents, so it will be in the children until regenerated. Thus the natural is developed first, as St. Paul tells us, "It is first the natural and then the spiritual." It is said that in Jesus there was neither male nor female, but both were one in Christ. We are by the natural law of God born either male or female, but when we are born of the spirit we are in oneness of spirit, which is one with God; therefore we are in harmony with the principles of God in the male as we are in the female, on the pure principle of mother-love.

It is impossible for a true mother to love her son more than her daughter, or the daughter more than the son. These two children are a part of her own life; therefore when we are born of God we love all flesh, although the flesh does not love the spirit of God in us any more than it did in Jesus, but persecutes us as it did Him. Yet you can say, as He did, "Father, forgive them for they know not what they do."

It is the Holy Spirit which comes to save soul and body, to enlighten the world, not to condemn it, and to destroy the works of darkness and ignorance by the light of love and truth. This is the light of the spirit which lighteth every man that cometh into this world. This is why Jesus was called, "The Light of the world." Therefore when ye are born of God ye are called, "the lights of the world," "a city set upon a hill." When we are thus spiritually enlightened we will clearly see that the head of every one born of God, has the mind of Christ, and His lamb-like gentleness corresponding to the first constellation sign, Aries, having also the strength of Taurus in the neck, the light of the spirit in the face, as the Pleiades lights up the eye and face of Taurus, the Bull, the second sign of the Zodiacal belt of the Heavens. This gives us Gemini, the arms, as the third sign, Cancer, the breast, the fourth, Leo, the heart, the fifth, Virgo, the bowels, the sixth, and Libra, the reins, as the seventh. These are the seven natural mountains on which the woman of Babylon has set up her kingdom, the lusts of the flesh enthroned thereon; but the soul born of God can now look at Babylon, the doomed city, as fallen, and her seven natural kings, accompanied by the eighth, going into perdition.

The Lamb, the Christ-spirit in us, having overcome the beast according to the promise, "To him
that overcometh will I give to sit with me on my
throne, as I, through overcoming, sit with my Father
on His throne."

Before we take up the ninth constellation, we will
look a little further at Scorpio, the supposed cause
of the curse, the representative serpent, the cause
of almost all the natural evil since the days of
Adam and Eve.

Scorpio, the eighth sign in the Heavens, has, as we
have shown, its correspondence in the human nature
in the secrets. This is the great human center of
propagation, but owing to the low order of thought
in the human mind, we find that the natural scorpio
is a monster in the shape of a human parasite, and
that through this great magnetic centre men and
women sin against themselves and others. Jesus said
"Whosoever looketh on a women to lust after her
in his heart hath committed adultery already."

All who walk after the flesh have this serpent to
contend with in themselves and others, until they are
delivered from this body of death, and realize in
themselves, with St. Paul in the 8th chapter of
Romans, "There is therefore now no condemna-
tion to those who are in Christ Jesus, who walk not

after the flesh but after the spirit, for the law of
the spirit of life in Christ Jesus hath made me free
from the law of sin and death." This is the new birth
of the spirit, the second coming of Christ to man and
woman. Christ is God, and the spirit of God first enters through the law of procreation, in conception.
God is love, is life, and thus the law of the spirit of life
in conception contains all the attributes of God in
itself. There are certain laws of unfoldment which
are requisite to a full development of that life in
its dual form, in its spiritual oneness with God.
Hence the germ of eternal life is first sown in the
natural body, and when quickened it assumes its spiritual body—its incorruptible body. The head, the seat
of the senses, is the first form of infant creation.
From the head the different forms and parts of the
body shoot out into a perfect whole.

Then, and not until then, is the mother conscious
of life in her child; thus we find that the womb of
woman is the cradle of God, where His thoughts
take form and shape. The first thought is the
motion of life in the child which speaks to the
mother, saying, " Here am I; prepare ye a place for
me, that when I come forth ye may be ready to receive me." Few mothers realize the charge which
is given them to keep, and that the spirit of life,

love and truth comes to them as a helpless infant to be naturally nourished, trained and taught. Hence motherhood is the direct avenue through which the world is blessed with pure, true and holy lives, or cursed by their opposites. We can come to only one conclusion, which is, that the first order of creation, the law of life. is as perfect to-day as in the beginning. Human civilization has not changed nor improved the original plan of creation given in the procreative law.

Darwin and others claim that man came originally from the monkey and baboon species; but neither monkeys nor baboons produce men We know that each type or form of life will repeat itself; but from man and woman, however animal they are inclined to be, their offspring will walk on two feet instead of four. Much more might be said of the evils of the natural Scorpio and its tendency to grossness in the human family. On the other hand let us contemplate the powerful influence of this heavenly sign when it is revealed in the human family, in its spiritual order. Truly, then we shall have born to us Samuels, Jeremiahs, and Johns; yea, sainted and holy men and women, of Godly love and wisdom.

SAGITTARIUS, OR THE ARCHER.

Sagittarius, the ninth Constellation sign, is the next in order. This sign is represented in the heavens as a bowman with an arrow. He is half man and half horse, armed with a bow and quiver. We find this sign in the heavens corresponding with the natural man in the thighs, indicating the strength and swiftness of the horse, with the sharp shooting tendency of the human mind; also the cupidity and cunning of the hunter, who aims often at the thighs and limbs in pointing at his prey, so as to maim rather than to kill outright. The natural man has all the elements of this sign. Some lie in wait for their prey, not caring whether their arrow strikes the head or feet so that they hit the mark aimed at. If the natural man has this sign largely developed in his nature, he carries and uses his pistol or whatever weapon he may find at hand when occasion calls it forth. Hence the natural man is like Ishmael, his hand being raised against every man and every man's hand against him. On the other hand we read that " He who dwelleth in the secret place of the Most High, abideth under the shadow of the Almighty.

Such have nothing to fear from the arrow that

flieth by day. "Thou shalt not be afraid of the
terror by night, nor the pestilence that walketh in
darkness, nor the destruction that wasteth at
noon day." "A thousand may fall by thy side and
ten thousand at thy right hand, but it shall not
come nigh to thee ; because thou hast made the
Lord thy refuge, even the Most High thy habitation.
There shall no evil befall thee, neither shall any
plague come nigh thy dwelling, for He shall give
His angels charge over thee to keep thee in all thy
ways." This Psalm makes clear the spiritual correspondence of the ninth Constellation sign, that if
born of the spirit we have nothing to fear from the
natural Sagittarius, because we have made the
Lord our refuge. Our natural life is in harmony
with the spiritual signs and order of the Heavens,

CAPRICORNUS, THE GOAT.

Capricornus, or the Goat sign, is the tenth Constellation. This sign holds its correspondence in the
knees of men. The natural man born in this sign
is naturally high-minded and head-strong almost to
stubbornness. Like the goat, he will fight if you
undertake to drive or force him in a path that he
does not wish to take. We see very little difference

between the obstinacy of the billy goat and the nanny goat. There are very many people who live in the goat sign, who fight with their heads, who are slow in getting the consent of their human will to agree with the sentiments of their heart, being high-minded, heady and erratic. It is hard for them to meekly bend their knees. We see a great deal of this spiritual wickedness in high places. Yet God said, " Every knee shall bow and every tongue confess."

Although it is difficult for those who naturally belong to the goat sign to yield their will to God's, still the thought that " all shall know Him in time" comforts us, although we see very great wrestling between the spirit and the flesh. Often we see the results of the struggle in stiff and swollen joints, weak knees, rheumatic affliction and dropsical tendencies, the result largely of uncontrolled will in those who would rather live on the mountain of self-indulgence than come down into the valley of humiliation and submission to the will of God. But, nevertheless, one thing is certain ; the goat, or animal, in our nature has to be surrendered to God, for, until it is done, there will be inharmony between the brain and the body, and while this state exists there will be sickness. For mankind to be healthy and happy Christ must be the head, then every member of the body will gladly obey the head. This gives peace and good will to the natural man, and glory, majesty and power to the spiritual man.

Christ works in and through the human nature for the uplifting of the individual soul in Godliness, making the Lord's prayer practical, " Thy will be done in the Earth as in Heaven." This heavenly consellation sign Capricornus shows us that while the head and the knees are represented in the goat sign, the hinder parts of the goat are like those of a fish, correspondingly connecting this tenth sign with the eleventh and the twelfth signs Aquarius and Pisces, or Fishes. Here we find the opposite tendency from the high-headed aspirations of the goat to the other extremes of life's creations, which live in the sea and marshy lands and waters. These are represented in the limbs and feet of the natural man and woman in the eleventh and twelfth Constellations, correspondingly connecting them with the creation of life in the sea, from the smallest fish to the largest whale, and in the firmament of the heavens ; revealing to us how man and women are held by the laws of attraction to the starry heavens, and also by the laws of gravitation to the very depth of the ocean, to the centre of the Earth ;

and the natural central office of these laws is in each one individually. This central office is the centre of the centripetal, located in and around the umbilical cord, the ring and the region of the Virgo, or Virgin, centre of life. By and through this life principle man is enabled to go down into the depths, and up to the heights, and also to all the lengths and breadths of God's universe.

AQUARIUS, OR THE WATER-BEARER.

Aquarius, the eleventh Constellation sign, is represented in the heavens as a man with water pouring or flowing from an urn, yet spiritually discerned it is from the abdominal centre. Man thus represents both male and female in the Lord. This is confirmed by the word of Jesus, (He who believeth in me, out of his belly shall flow rivers of living water.

The sign of the water-bearer proves that from the Virgo-center of human life flow the waters of life. This might be called God's earthly dipper. We know that the mother's life flows to her child until formed in the womb, until *she breathes it forth a living Soul.* This interior life flows outward also through the intermediate and exterior life-center, Virgo. Sometimes this inner fountain overflows and gushes through every pore and avenue of the whole'individual nature.   But Virgo is the center of the law of attraction, where the human meets the human, and the currents of life are exchanged by the more harmonious and abundant one supplying the want in the weaker one.   This is the law of love, "Bear ye one another's burdens and so fulfil the law."

This is the true method of healing.   This is the transmission of love; the transfusion of blood. Blood is the life of the word.   Jesus gave His body and blood to save the life of humanity, yet we have cause to draw a very dark picture of the natural exchange which now exists in the human family : the carnal relations of man and woman on the earth are the opposites of this holier life-giving power.

Mothers give their life to their offspring in pregnancy, but that life consists largely of carnal thoughts, and desires, love of self, pride of intellect, love of the body and excessive care for the things of this world, the sexual things, all of which weigh down the soul and chain it to the earth, and the spirit and every divine principle is set at nought. From such parents come only what they can give. Nature repeats itself always. On the same principle, such men and women give to those with whom they associate the natural spirit of the flesh, and this element carries always with it sorrow, sickness

and death, because it is carnal and must pass away
—Hence the necessity of living spiritually, that we
may carry wherever we go, the seeds of truth, the
water of life, which gives life and destroys death.
Spirit is life ; yea, life eternal.

Thus we see that the pure, spiritual mother holds
the power of transmitting to her sons and daughters
life eternal, bringing forth Water-bearers who will
always walk in the light of the spirit of the constellations, not alone in the light of Aquarius, but in the
full light of the twelve, making them " the lights of
this world ; " Cities set upon a hill ; Christ in you the
hope of glory. Thus male and female can in the spirit
return to their Eden state, with the knowledge
of the truth of life flowing from them in word and
works as living fountains, wells of truth, watering
the gardens of God's vineyard here below, where
much of His life in its germinal state has never yet
seen the sun-light of day.

The history of the future will record Christ men
and women, who by their example and exhibiton of
perfection, in the knowledge of the law and order of
a wise Creator, will clearly reveal the systems
of His creations.

When the veil of flesh is lifted from the hearts
and minds of humanity, there will be an irresistible

drawing of all souls unto Him. "If I be lifted up," said Jesus, "I will draw all men unto me." When Jesus is revealed in Christ, all will be able to see themselves as they are and choose, if they will, whom they will serve; then they will see God as a God of love, who does not create and after a brief caress repudiate and disown. No, no; ignorance and disobedience has painted a horrible picture of the divine and merciful father, whose love is more tender than a mother's love.

Can a mother forget her suckling child? No, she cannot; for the child's cry for food pierces the mother's breast. So the cry of the child of earth penetrates the heart of its God, and we are never forgotten. But we may, like pouting children, go off in a corner, and cry and sob, and say God has forsaken us.

No, no, child of earth; "*Come to me, come to me,*" is the call of God, "*and I will give you rest.*"

Christ is God; He has never left His people. How could God leave Himself when He created man in His own image male and female? But man through disobedience and ignorance has left God.

The life of man is the breath of God. God breathed into man the breath of life and he became a living soul. "The Lord breathed upon His disciples, and said, Receive ye the Holy Ghost." "O breath, breathe upon these slain, that they may live." As the valley of dry bones were breathed upon and they lived. God is called the breath of the nostrils. The way of the breath of life. Man must have a dull nostril not to perceive that when He ceases to have power to inhale or exhale, the opposite of life, the enemy of man, has presented his claim—Death, which robs the man of his free will to live, which God gave to man when He gave him his life.

O man, know thyself! Yet man cannot possibly know himself, until he first knows God. Then he cannot know God, without knowing himself. John said, " Now we know that we are the sons of God, because we have His spirit witnessing with ours." Multitudes, nations, tongues and people, will yet say as John said—" Now we know that we are the sons of God, because we have God's spirit witnessing with ours "—as the voice of God in oneness of spirit will yet cover the earth as the waters covers the sea. Christ the revealed life of humanity in the earth and in the Heavens, will reveal Himself in this the closing cycle of time.

PISCES, OR FISHES.

Pisces, or Fishes, the twelfth Constellation. This sign symbolizes the elements of the sea-born queen of love. The Mermaid coming up out of her watery grave, her earth-bound home, with her fruitful issues of sea and land. The treasure of the inner life. The kingdom of the soul.

Woman has been hidden in the depths; her life, her Eve nature, has been under bondage to the curse. She has indeed been chained to her own earthly affections. She might well be called Marah, for the wells of her soul have been made bitter. The waters of the world have flown into the pure streams of her life. The surface streams of natural life have almost buried the well of living water in her innermost nature out of sight—that from which she has drawn her vital life; her motherhood in God. Oh Marah, Mother Eve! the water of thy life is the written word, the little book which John ate, which was in his mouth sweet, but in his belly bitter. The spirit of life in the word is sweet, but the living out of that word in love brings the bitterness, the cruci- fixions. But the crucifixions of the flesh bring out into the full light of day, the spirit of God in

woman. This spirit of God in woman, given to the
world through woman, needs to be clearly understood, that the Christ spirit shall no longer be
covered with error, superstition and bigotry.

Woman as the fallen Eve, has been traduced and
looked upon as the author of our womanly weaknesses
and our tendency to fall.   Mary, the redeemed Eve,
the mother of Jesus, has also suffered through the
human impossibility to understand how she could
be the wife of Joseph, and the spouse of the Holy
Ghost. But the revealed Christ unveils the truth
and tears away all the coverings of earthly prejudice,
with the ignorance of the past, and all the hin-
drances to a oneness of spirit in understanding, God
in spirit and in truth.   We have already shown the
spirit of the Heavens ; the mother from the Pleiades ;
she who is the mother of all living ; the effeminate
nature of God ; the one to whom the Creator said
"Let us make man in our own image, male and female." Adam and Eve were made, blest and sent forth
to bring forth.   The natural partook of the natural,
and the spirit of the Heavens was lost in material fog,
and is to this day.

The natural cannot discern spirit. It reasons,
speculates and fails. It is only the spirit of the Divine
that reveals the Divine—and until the human soul is

willing to be taught, willing to be still and know God,
the Divine cannot reveal the Divine. Hence the required submission of the human will to God's will.
This human will is naturally located in the brain. But
when it is surrendered to God, it is united with Him
in the maternal center of the human being. The
human will in the brain is to the human what the
wheelhouse is to the ship, but the dual will
is where the spirit and the human soul meet
and unite as one life and one mind. This will-cen-
ter is the Solar Plexus, the maternal center of the
spiritual sun of the soul, where Libra and Virgo
meet. This is the solar center of the solar system of
the human soul of man, and woman. Let it be understood that it is from woman man receives his
spiritual love : his natural love comes from natural
life, but his spiritual love is from his mother. For
example, if a son is more like his natural father
in temperament than his mother, he will live in
the natural intellect or reasoning faculties. But
if the son has his mother's nature predominating,
and she being a godly woman, from the son, as
well as from the daughter of such a mother, the
light of her spirit will shine forth as the solar
rays of the light of Heaven, and all who come in
contact with the children of such mothers will

feel the Holy influence of a Holy Spirit, a Holy
Mary, a Holy Jesus, a Holiness which is whole.
ness in Christ, a oneness in God, a meek and lowly
Nazarene. One who stoops to the lowest soul and
lifts it up. One who ascends to the highest heaven.
One who, whether in the lowest hell or the highest
heaven is one in and with God. This is Christ
revealed in the earthly form of man and woman. Al
made in his image may attain to this state. All may
know him from the youngest to the oldest on the
earth, who are willing to leave the earthly loves for
the heavenly. They may become perfect even as the
Heavenly Father is perfect.

God said, "Come buy of me Gold tried in the Fire."
We are in that day, or nearing it, when nothing but
the pure Gold the Spirit of the Word, will be in use.
Before the close of the sign Pisces or Fishes it will
come to pass. We find that this constellation sign
in the heavens is correspondingly located in the
human feet. This spiritually reveals the words of
Jesus to Peter when He was about to wash Peter's
feet, and Peter said unto Jesus, Thou shalt never
wash my feet. Jesus answered him, "If I wash
thee not thou hast no part with me; he that is
washed needeth not save to wash his feet, and is
clean every whit."

The knowledge contained in the words of Jesus to Peter, John 13, is disclosed in the twelfth Constellation. Jesus said to Peter after He had washed his feet, Ye are clean but not all. Jesus knowing that Peter could not come into the fullness of the truth, until the fullness of time. The close of the twelfth cycle.

Paul tell us in the 8th of Romans that the earnest expectations of the Creature waiteth for the manifestation of the sons of God. For we know, said Paul, that the whole creation groaneth and travaileth in pain together until now ; and not only they, but we ourselves which have the first fruit of the Spirit. Even we ourselves groan within ourselves, waiting for the adoption, to wit, the redemption of our body, for we are saved by hope ; but hope that is seen is not hope. But if we hope for that we see not, then do we with patience wait for it.

Paul states clearly in the 21st verse of this chapter, what this hope is, he says, " Because the creature itself shall be delivered from the bondage of corruption, into the glorious liberty of the children of God." Thus the truth that was manifest in Jesus, the Christ, and the first fruits of that truth left within the Christian Church in the morning of that day, is to be revealed

in this the closing age.   As we have passed through
that day and almost the night, so that the new day
is dawning to which Paul looked forward so
earnestly.   Truth redeemed from error will bring
redemption to the souls and bodies of the children
of men.   God is truth, and Christ is God, and God
is love.   Thus Christ, the God of love, alone cleanses
and washes away all our sins.

When we are like Peter, willing He should wash
not alone our feet, but our head and hands also,
Christ is the spirit of truth which leads in to all
truth.   He alone can reveal the past and its relation
to the present and the future.   He alone can in-
terpret and teach us how we are to understand the
flying roll, to which the angel of God called Zacariah's
attention.   [Zacariah V.]   The flying roll is the
knowledge of the curse going forth over the whole
earth, revealing the lead which this curse placed on
the lips of women.   This chapter also shows the
lifting of the curse, the unveiling of the truth.

"And behold there came out two woman, and the
wind was in their wings, for they had wings like the
wings of a stork; and they lifted up the Ephah between the Earth and the Heavens.   Then said I to
the angel that talked with me, Whither do these
bare the Ephah?   And he said to me, To build it a

house in the land of Shinar and it shall be established on it own base."

Truth crushed to earth shall rise again. It shall
be set on its own base. " This mortal must put on
immortality. Then shall be brought to pass the saying that is written, Death is swallowed up in victory.
O death where is thy sting, O grave where is thy
victory. The sting of death is sin. But thanks
be to God who giveth the victory through our Lord
Jesus Christ," 1 Cor. 15.

This victory over death, this human completeness in God, is Christ revealed in His Divine
humanity. The very same Christ which raised
Jesus from the dead. The very same Christ Jesus
whom the Apostles saw go up into heaven, and
a cloud receive Him out of their sight. The same
Jesus Christ which the Angel said would return to
the earth in like manner as they saw Him go up into
Heaven. The Christ Spirit never left the earth
since the creation, save in Jesus the redeemed son,
the first born of many generations.

That which is born of the earth is earthly
and is held to the earth by earthly ties or
natural and spiritual laws, until God's Spirit of
love and wisdom is made manifest in the human,
until the image of the Divine is made fully mani-

fest, until the image of the Heavenly is revealed in the earthly. True, there are recorded transactions, Enoch, Elijah and others, but there is only one son who has as yet attained to the image of His Creator—The man-God.

The Holy Spirit, the Comforter, has been made manifest in all ages. But the fullness of the revealed Christ was only lived out in the will and wisdom of the Father on this earth, in Jesus. In him law became love, and love was the fullfilling of the law. When we attain to this, we shall be like Him; and then we shall see Him as He is, Lord God Almighty, Maker of heaven and earth.

THE NUMERICAL LANGUAGE
OF SOUNDS.

THE KEY TO UNIVERSAL HARMONY. THE SOCIAL SYMPH-
ANY EXISTING BETWEEN THE HEAVENS
AND THE EARTH.

THE law of musical harmony which exists between the Twelve Constellation signs in the zodiacal Heavens and the human body is in the common order of time. It sounds and runs as follows:

One, and one, and one.

Two, and two, and two.

Three, and three, and three.

Four, and four, and four.

Five, and five, and five.

Six, and six, and six.

Seven, and seven, and seven.

Eight, and eight, and eight.

Nine, and nine, and nine.

Ten, and ten, and ten.

Eleven, and eleven, and eleven.

Twelve, and twelve, and twelve.

These are the twelve corresponding sounds in the twelve constellations, each number harmonizing itself; and they together are the regulators of the same order of sounds. These are also the numerical languages of all sounds, so that when one has learned to designate one sound from the other, having mastered this knowledge of sounds in all their bearings, one will be able to converse in all languages composed of sounds. Everything in nature speaks its own tongue, and those educated by the Spirit of the God of nature will converse with all emanations of life ; they will have the gift of tongues. Realizing fully that all that which lives, lives unto itself, and yet lives for others also, as nothing comes from nothing, each has its own separate life although a part of the whole.

But each must be understood for itself, so as to place it where it belongs in the scale of sounds. The three times three time music embraces the threefold nature of man and woman in the Divine.

This musical knowledge harmonizes intelligently all the relations of man with man, and man with his creator, God.

The human intellectual knowledge of music is largely mingled with the crude idea of Godly sentiment. Thus while it may be masterly in its execution, in voice culture and vocal power, also in the masterly touch on and over stringed instruments, nevertheless, while the human skill and effort deserves appreciation there remains still the fact, that the Godly sentiment of soul power is missing, and that is the greater part; the part that touches the soul of all, and carries an awakening power through the whole soul of nature.

The musical scale of sounds consists of twelve cadences. These twelve cadences are composed of articulate and inarticulate sounds, comprised in the vibration of sounds; and through the twelve cords in music the full expression of all these sounds can be learned and mastered completely.

The arms and hands have their sounds in their musical movements, which can be readily learned, the left differing from the right.

The knees and feet are also musically represented. When the head is due South, the shoulders, elbows and hands are the south-eastern and south-western points of the compass.

The feet, knees and haunches represent the horizontal lines of the north, and the north-eastern and western points of the compass.

When the individual stands or lies on the due south and north line of demarkation, the body from the neck to the groins represents the earth as it revolves around the Sun. The natural body is the counterpart of the Earth, and when we attain to the knowledge of our own human nature, we will be enabled to comprehend the earth's surface and its interior. The human body is as fully intended by the creator to revolve in ·its own orbit, as the earth is to revolve around the sun once in twenty-four hours. The individual mind is, or should be, a sun in its relation to its own body, and when one understands one's own soul-nature one will realize that there is in all a spiritual Solar Plexus from which radiates a reflex action, a life motor, a central sun, from which center all one's human nature may receive its perpetual life, and if understood fully, the external or corporeal life of the body, need never know death.

When we have the mind of Christ, we will know these things; we will be central suns, proving individually the perfect law and order of God in human form. This very life-principle in the human when made manifest in the earth, will prove the perfect law and order which causes the earth to revolve around the central sun of its own attraction, hence its own existence. Thus the individuals who understand their own spiritual and natural powers, will cause their own physical body to perform its own functions with perfect regularity and precision. The brain being the wheel-house, log-book and compass, by and through which the perfect mind of the navigator becomes a self-propellor.

The ancients attained this knowledge. Their

method and system was founded on the mathematical calculation of distances, especially the distance from the moon to the sun at all hours of day and night. This mathematical knowledge, when put to practical use, brings the human body at all times subject to motion, when the correct distances are applied to the lungs and air tubes, and valves of the heart.

The human mind understanding its own human nature, its corporeal body can at will propel, condense and transform itself, and transmit its power mentally and physically to all distances. Jesus attained to this personal perfection in Himself; attained to it in the will of the Father: and His spirit inspires and evokes all to come to the same perfection in the Father which He attained, which is all knowledge in love; and knowledge in love gives the power of wisdom. Jesus said, " Be ye perfect even as your Father in Heaven is perfect." Christ Jesus .would not have said this were it impossible to attain to this perfection, and He made the way of life, the path of this perfection possible. He said further, " I will ask the Father and He will send you another comfortor, teacher, who will abide with you for ever, the spirit of truth who will lead you into all truth." " Is not this the Christ ? "—The Comforter who is leading us into all truth, and revealing all truth to those who are hungering 'and thirsting for it ?

When the twelve chords in music correspond musically to the twelve signs of the Zodiac, and are applied to the different parts of the human body, and are truly designated chronologically, which is time properly proportioned, then each member of the body will be in harmony with itself, in unity one member with the other. Christ will be the head of each one, and Christ is God. When this musical harmony exists in one soul, or in many souls, time with them will be music, and music will be time. Hence the restriction of earthly time and space will be overcome. The law and order of the Heavens is established in the human nature of the one or many who have attained thereto. This is being hid with Christ in God. It is the peace which passeth not away. It is the eternal oneness; the Nirvana of the Buddist. It is the ever-present and eternal now of the Christian. The God of law and order. The infinite presence of the Peace-maker, reconciling the finite with the infinite relations of spirit with matter, where order, Heaven's first law, is established in love, love is life eternal, and time and music is love's existence.

This state of spiritual existence communes with all creation through sound, each speaking its own language, yet the language of each does musically apply itself understandingly to all life and all grades of life's unfoldment. When this is perfectly under-

stood there will be a musical harmony existing between the earthly musician and the Heavenly Choir.
The earthly musician in this school of thought will be
in harmony with the music of the planetary worlds
and the music of the one will be heard in the other.
There will be sacred concerts on the earth which will
seem to those present as if old things had passed
away, and the new Heavens and the new earth wherein dwells righteousness had taken their place, and that
the kingdoms of this world were indeed the kingdoms
if our Lord Jesus Christ, where the Hosannas are
sung in all their fullness.

These sweet singers of Israel will see as John saw
in the Isle of Patmos—"A lamb standing on Mount
Zion, and with Him a hundred and forty and four
thousand, having His Father's name written on their
foreheads. And I heard a voice from Heaven, as the
voice of a great thunder; and the voice of harpers
harping with their harps, singing the new song before
the throne, and before the Elders. And no one could
learn that song but the one hundred and forty and
four thousand, who were redeemed from the earth.
Those also who stood on the sea of glass, the mirror
of truth; having the harps of God, singing the songs
of Moses, the servant of God and the Lamb, saying:
great and marvelous are thy works, Lord God Almighty; just and true are thy ways, Thou King of

Saints!" Christ revealed in the heavens, brings up the redeemed of the earth; with joyful songs of praise. Singing, O Earthly joy; O Heavenly peace; our ransomed souls implore.

The rising generation to accept the truth, the open door. "The Christ of God." "The Sent."— "The Deliverer of His People." "The Immanuel God with us.

THE END.